EXTREME

Body Bugs

Uninvited Guests on Your Body

Trevor Day

Capstone

Fact Finders is published by Capstone Press,
a Capstone Publishers company.
151 Good Counsel Drive, P.O. Box 669,
Mankato, Minnesota 56002.
www.capstonepress.com

First published 2008

Produced for A & C Black by

Monkey Puzzle Media Ltd
48 York Avenue, Hove
East Sussex BN3 1PJ, UK

Library of Congress Cataloging-in-Publication Data

Day, Trevor.
    Body bugs : uninvited guests on your body / Trevor Day.
        p. cm. -- (Fact finders. Extreme!)
    Includes bibliographical references and index.
    Summary: "Describes microorganisms and insects that
    live on and in the human body"--Provided by publisher.
    ISBN-13: 978-1-4296-3112-9 (hardcover)
    ISBN-10: 1-4296-3112-0 (hardcover)
    ISBN-13: 978-1-4296-3132-7 (softcover)
    ISBN-10: 1-4296-3132-5 (softcover)
    1. Microorganisms--Juvenile literature. I. Title. II. Series.

QR57.D38 2009
579--dc22

2008025523

Printed in China

102009
005541

Editor: Steve Parker
Design: Mayer Media Ltd
Picture research: Laura Barwick
Series consultant: Jane Turner

This book is produced using paper that is made from wood
grown in managed, sustainable forests. It is natural,
renewable, and recyclable. The logging and manufacturing
processes conform to the environmental regulations of the
country of origin.

Picture acknowledgements
Alamy p. 6 (Phototake Inc); Bridgeman Art Library
p. 26 (Archives Charmet); Corbis pp. 4 bottom
(MedicalRF.com), 14 top (Visuals Unlimited), 14 bottom
(image100), 17 (Mediscan), 19 (Visuals Unlimited), 20
(CDC/PHIL); Getty Images p. 5 (Mark Scott), 8 (David
Scharf), 12 (Hepp), 13 (Wolf Fahrenbach), 15 (Dr. David M.
Phillips), 18 (Nicole Duplaix/National Geographic),
29 (Jan Greune); Science Photo Library pp. 1 (National
Cancer Institute), 4 top (Andrew Syred), 7 (Steve
Gschmeissner), 9, 10 (Dr. Steve Patterson), 11 (Dr. John
Brackenbury), 16 (Scott Camazine), 21 (Eye of Science), 23
(National Cancer Institute), 24 top (Eye of Science),
24 bottom (Eric Grave), 25 (CNRI), 28; Still Pictures
pp. 22 (Darlyne A. Murawski), 27 (Mark Edwards).

The front cover shows a picture of a human head louse
taken through a powerful microscope (Science Photo
Library/Photo Insolité Realité).

Every effort has been made to contact copyright holders of
material reproduced in this book. Any omissions will be
rectified in subsequent printings if notice is given to the
publishers.

CONTENTS

Abbreviations **m** stands for meters • **ft** stands for feet • **in** stands for inches • **cm** stands for centimeters • **km/h** stands for kilometers per hour • **mph** stands for miles per hour

Open wide

Next time you're tempted to skip brushing your teeth, remember that you're encouraging the bugs that cause stinky breath and rotting teeth!

*Plaque is a gunky mixture of **bacteria** and rotting food on teeth that looks messy under the microscope.*

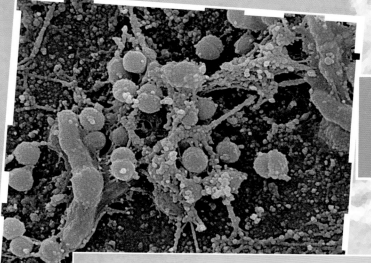

Gums become swollen and tender from acids and other bacterial chemicals.

Long in the teeth

This phrase means "getting old." It describes how the gums shrink back and expose more of the teeth in older people. It is caused by bacterial gum disease.

plaque mixture of bacteria, saliva, and rotting food that coats teeth and gums

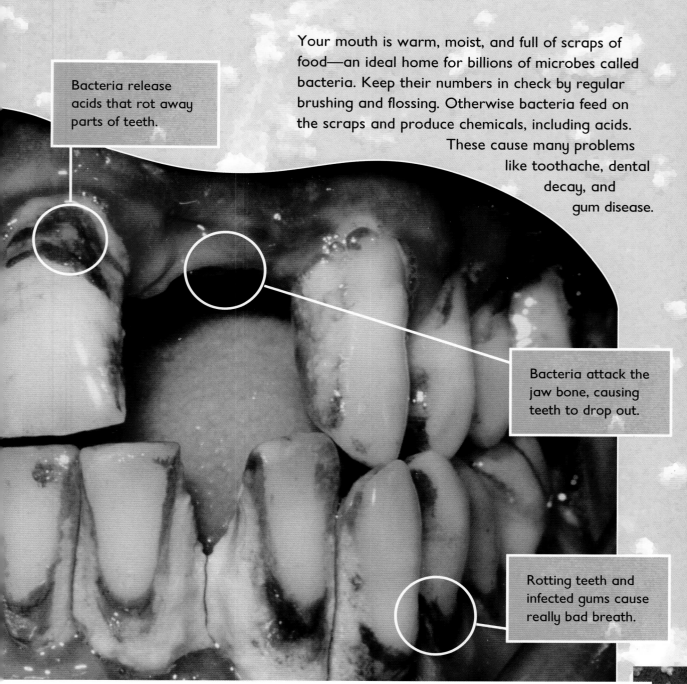

Bacteria release acids that rot away parts of teeth.

Your mouth is warm, moist, and full of scraps of food—an ideal home for billions of microbes called bacteria. Keep their numbers in check by regular brushing and flossing. Otherwise bacteria feed on the scraps and produce chemicals, including acids. These cause many problems like toothache, dental decay, and gum disease.

Bacteria attack the jaw bone, causing teeth to drop out.

Rotting teeth and infected gums cause really bad breath.

bacteria common small- to medium-sized microbes

Sniffing you out!

Each person has their own special smell. It's created by the blend of chemicals in their sweat plus a personal mix of microscopic body bugs growing in it!

Bacteria on skin feed on skin flakes and oils. As they grow in stale sweat, they create a stinky smell. We all leave an unseen trail of this odor wherever we go. Even if it is not obvious to us, dogs and some other animals can smell it. Of course, some people are much smellier than others.

*In adults, fresh sweat contains body chemicals called **pheromones**, that may attract people of the opposite sex.*

pheromone   chemical that has a smell that affects other people, without them being aware

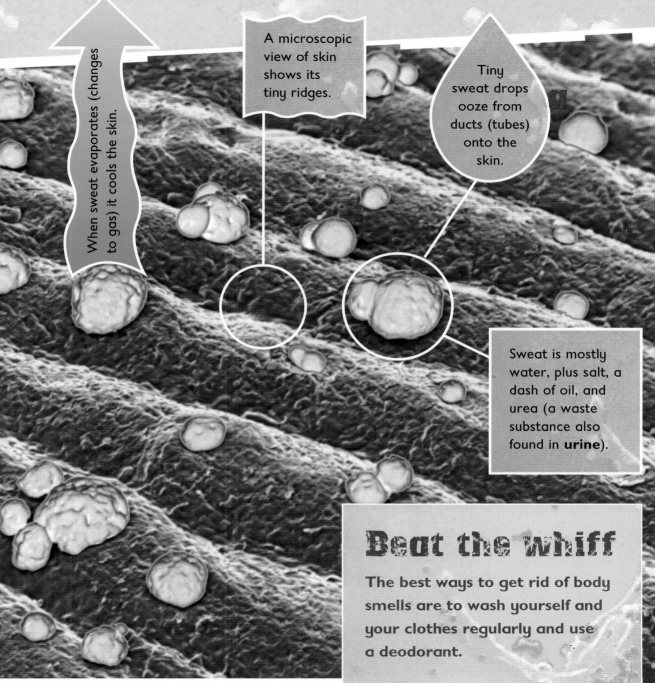

When sweat evaporates (changes to gas) it cools the skin.

A microscopic view of skin shows its tiny ridges.

Tiny sweat drops ooze from ducts (tubes) onto the skin.

Sweat is mostly water, plus salt, a dash of oil, and urea (a waste substance also found in **urine**).

Beat the whiff

The best ways to get rid of body smells are to wash yourself and your clothes regularly and use a deodorant.

urine person's liquid waste, also called pee

Fighting invasion!

Your body is always being bombarded by armies of microscopic bugs that try to sneak inside. But you have amazing defenses on the outside and inside to keep them at bay.

Your skin is your first line of defense. If a wound or cut lets bugs break through, you could be in trouble. Bacteria called *Staphylococcus* can cause blisters, blood poisoning, or even kill you.

BACTERIA BOUNCE OFF

Dead skin cells form a protective barrier that keeps out bacteria (shown here as pink dots). As old cells rub off, more cells from living layers below rise to take their place.

Pus is a pale ooze that forms at a wound and mixes with blood. It shows that white blood cells have been in action, killing bacteria.

pus pale liquid containing dead blood cells and bacteria

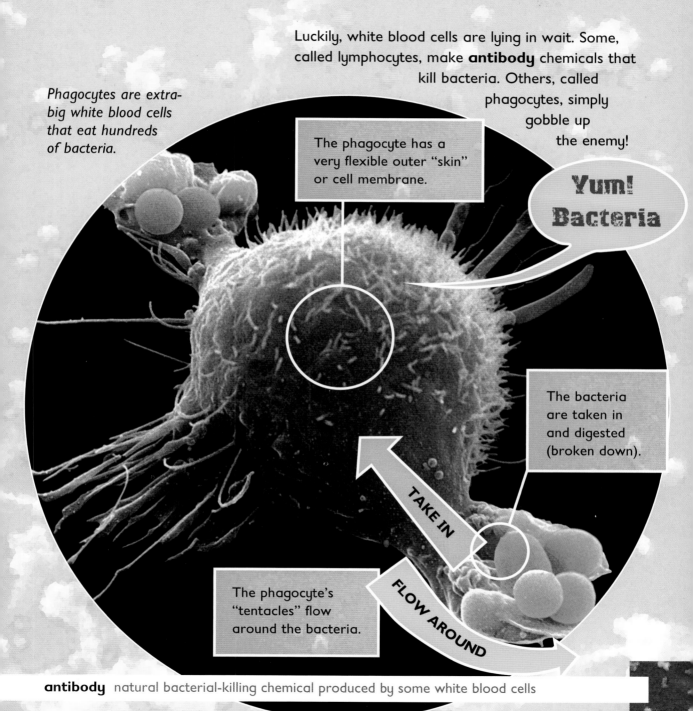

Luckily, white blood cells are lying in wait. Some, called lymphocytes, make **antibody** chemicals that kill bacteria. Others, called phagocytes, simply gobble up the enemy!

Phagocytes are extra-big white blood cells that eat hundreds of bacteria.

The phagocyte has a very flexible outer "skin" or cell membrane.

Yum! Bacteria

The bacteria are taken in and digested (broken down).

TAKE IN

FLOW AROUND

The phagocyte's "tentacles" flow around the bacteria.

antibody natural bacterial-killing chemical produced by some white blood cells

Ticked off

If you go down to the woods today ... be careful what latches onto you. It could be a blood-sucking tick.

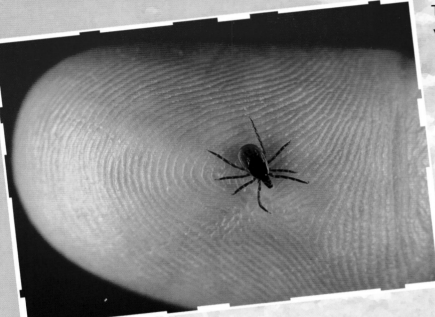

Ticks are not fussy about where they get their blood. A deer tick will just as happily feast on you as on a deer. The trouble is that you could catch a nasty disease in the process. It might be Lyme disease, or maybe Q **fever**, or even Rocky Mountain spotted fever, with **symptoms** like a red skin rash.

Ticks are eight-legged relatives of spiders. A hungry deer tick like this is the size of a match head. Its body swells about ten times larger after a blood meal.

Lyme disease

Effects of Lyme disease include reddening around the tick bite, followed by fever, headache and tiredness, aching muscles, and painful joints.

fever high body temperature

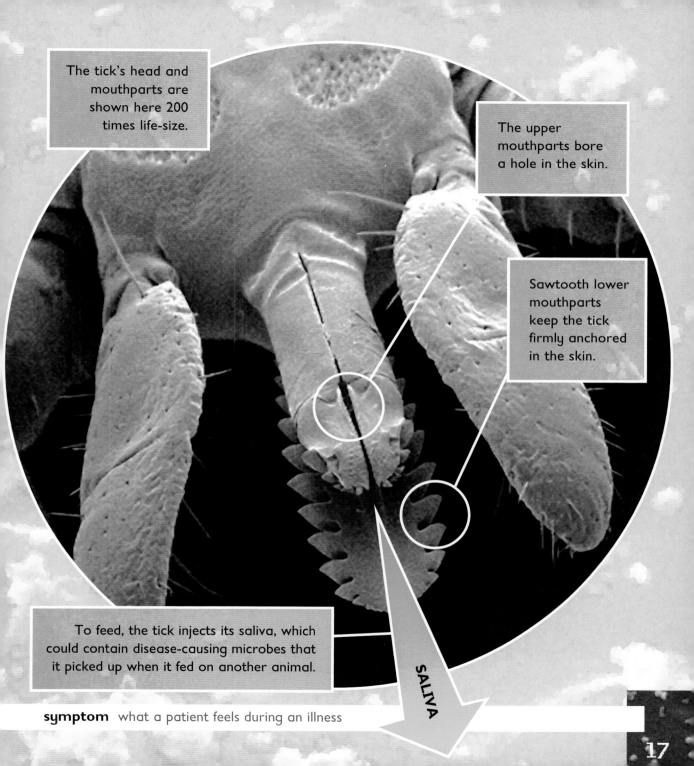

The tick's head and mouthparts are shown here 200 times life-size.

The upper mouthparts bore a hole in the skin.

Sawtooth lower mouthparts keep the tick firmly anchored in the skin.

To feed, the tick injects its saliva, which could contain disease-causing microbes that it picked up when it fed on another animal.

SALIVA

symptom what a patient feels during an illness

A flea in your ear

The Black Death

In Europe and Asia during the 1300s, about 50 million people died from a bacterial disease called bubonic **plague**—the Black Death. It was carried and spread by rat fleas.

What can jump 100 times its own body length, move objects 20,000 times its own weight, and has babies that eat their parents' poop? A flea!

Fleas are blood-sucking insects. Cats and dogs carry fleas, and humans have their own kind, too. Fleas have incredibly powerful legs and easily leap from one person to another. By harnessing the natural behavior of these insects, flea trainers can make them perform tricks in a miniature circus.

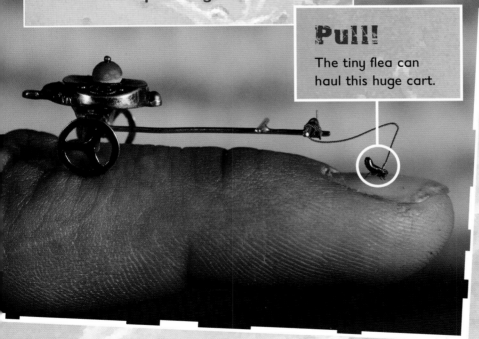

Pull!
The tiny flea can haul this huge cart.

Flea trainers put their performers to sleep briefly and tie them into miniature harnesses.

plague fast-spreading disease that kills people

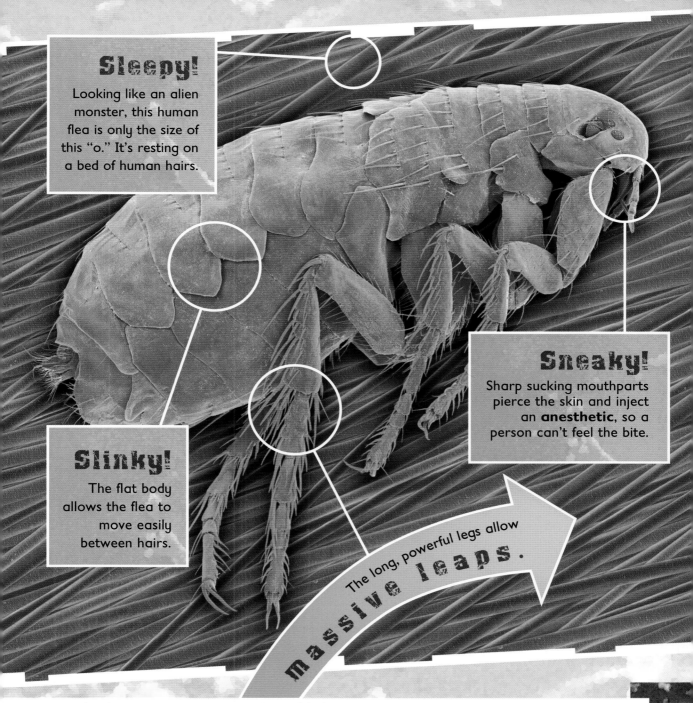

Sleepy!
Looking like an alien monster, this human flea is only the size of this "o." It's resting on a bed of human hairs.

Slinky!
The flat body allows the flea to move easily between hairs.

Sneaky!
Sharp sucking mouthparts pierce the skin and inject an **anesthetic**, so a person can't feel the bite.

The long, powerful legs allow **massive leaps.**

anesthetic substance that brings loss of feeling or consciousness

It's in the blood

One small sucker kills more than a million people a year. In some tropical countries, the mosquito's bite carries the deadly disease malaria.

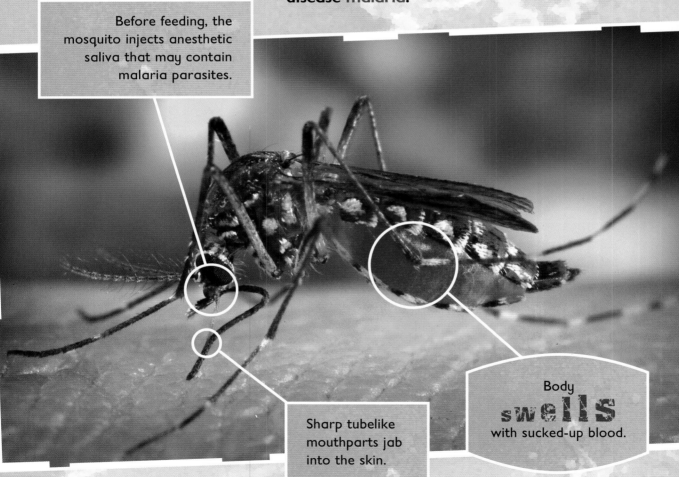

Before feeding, the mosquito injects anesthetic saliva that may contain malaria parasites.

Sharp tubelike mouthparts jab into the skin.

Body **swells** with sucked-up blood.

malaria dangerous disease caused by one-celled parasites transmitted through mosquito bites

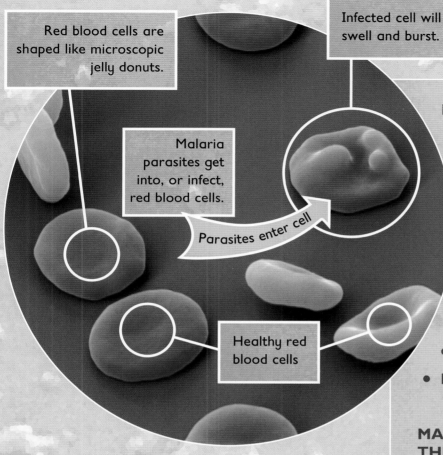

Red blood cells are shaped like microscopic jelly donuts.

Malaria parasites get into, or infect, red blood cells.

Infected cell will swell and burst.

Parasites enter cell

Healthy red blood cells

Inside the human body, malaria parasites enter red blood cells, where they grow and make the cells break open. This produces fever and chills.

Microbes called *Plasmodium* cause malaria. They are bigger than bacteria but smaller than this period. Malaria parasites spend part of their life inside a female mosquito. When she sucks a person's blood, she injects the parasites in her saliva.

FAMOUS MALARIA SUFFERERS INCLUDE:

- **Explorer Christopher Columbus**
- **Several U.S. presidents such as George Washington, Abraham Lincoln, and John F. Kennedy**
- **Actor Michael Caine**
- **Mother Teresa**

MALARIA KILLED THESE PEOPLE:

- **Alexander the Great**
- **Genghis Khan, the Mongol overlord**
- **Poet Lord Byron**

Boring worms

Swimmer's itch

Feeling your skin itch after a swim in a tropical lake or river could be a sign that boring worms have been at work!

Go swimming in a tropical river, and you might come home with some unwelcome guests—tiny young worms! They burrow into your skin, bore and tunnel through your flesh, and swim through your blood!

The disease **bilharzia** is caused by a wormy parasite called a blood fluke. Bilharzia affects more than 200 million people across the world. It is easily treated, but in poor places with little medical help, it kills several hundred thousand people each year.

In warm countries, tiny young flukes grow inside snails that live in still or slow-flowing fresh water. Then they leave the snails in search of people to infect.

bilharzia serious tropical disease caused by a fluke whose young bore through the skin

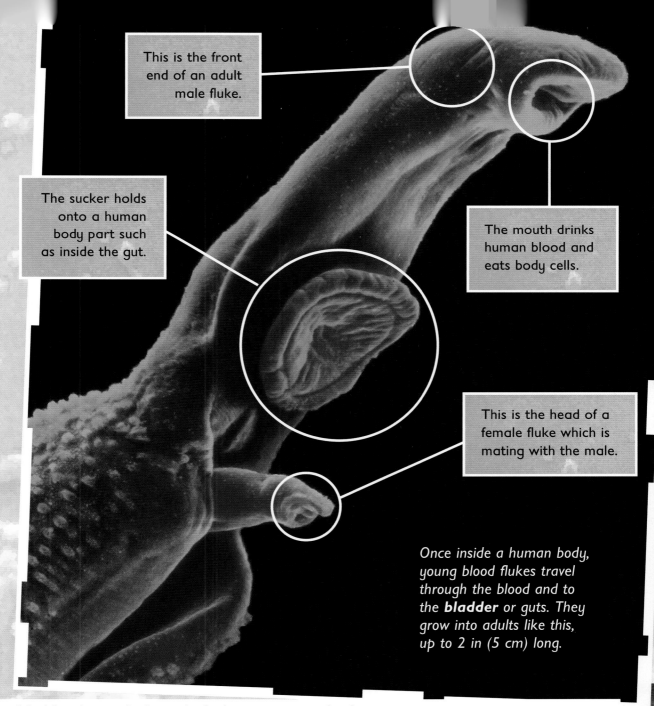

This is the front end of an adult male fluke.

The mouth drinks human blood and eats body cells.

The sucker holds onto a human body part such as inside the gut.

This is the head of a female fluke which is mating with the male.

*Once inside a human body, young blood flukes travel through the blood and to the **bladder** or guts. They grow into adults like this, up to 2 in (5 cm) long.*

bladder bag in the lower body that stores urine (pee)

Getting to the guts

Have you ever been sick or thrown up? This is usually a sign that you've eaten something that might contain nasty bugs or poisons!

People cook meat and fish for good reasons. It makes the food taste better than when it's raw. It also kills bugs hiding inside. Luckily, your stomach usually notices when you've eaten poisons or harmful bugs. It makes you vomit to try to get rid of them. But swallowed tapeworm eggs in undercooked meat or fish might get through the stomach to the intestine, where baby worms hatch out and grow.

The cells lining the stomach release acids and other chemicals that kill bugs.

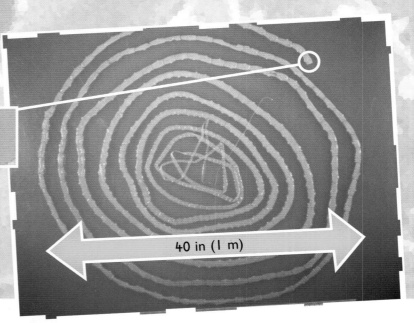

The tapeworm's head is the size of a pin head.

A human tapeworm can grow as long as 30 ft (9 m). It lives inside the intestine without the person noticing.

40 in (1 m)

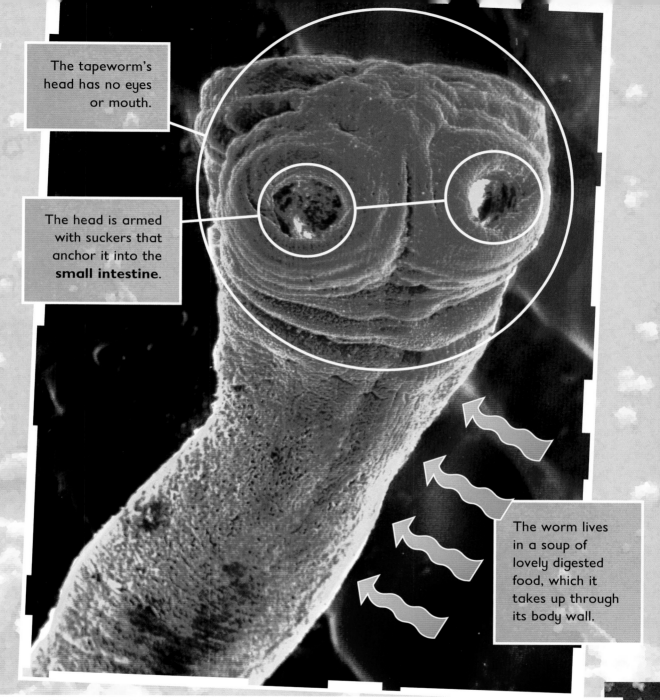

The tapeworm's head has no eyes or mouth.

The head is armed with suckers that anchor it into the **small intestine**.

The worm lives in a soup of lovely digested food, which it takes up through its body wall.

small intestine longest part of the gut, just after the stomach

25

What a waste!

Studying body wastes is a wonderfully smelly way to check a person for diseases and for any harmful bugs involved.

Scientists can tell a lot from body wastes. Using microscopes to study **feces** and urine, they can see dangerous tiny bugs or parasitic worms. Deadly diseases such as cholera and typhoid are caused by bacteria that live in the guts of infected people. These bacteria cause terrible **diarrhea** that drains life-giving fluids from the body.

LE MÉDECIN AUX URINES.

Before modern tests, doctors would try to identify a disease by studying the patient's urine, its color and smell—and its taste.

feces person's solid wastes, also called poop

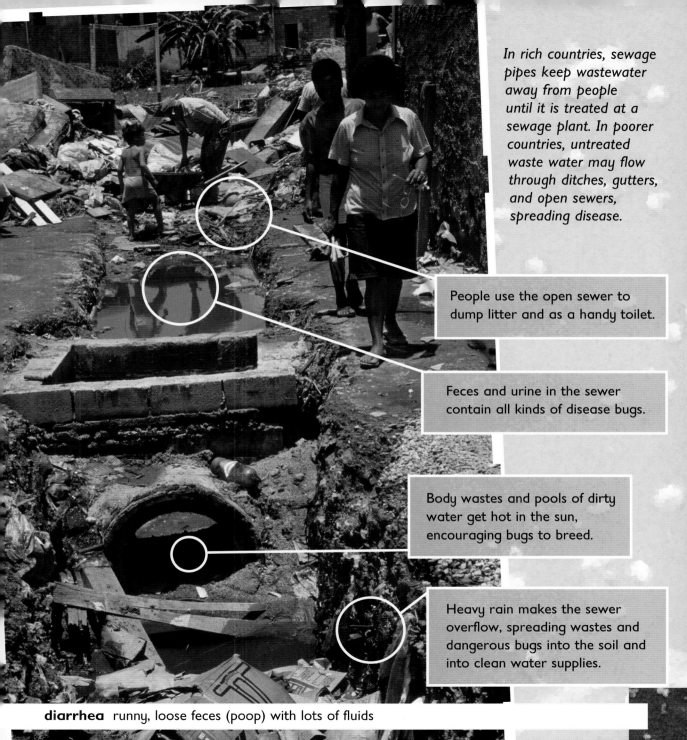

In rich countries, sewage pipes keep wastewater away from people until it is treated at a sewage plant. In poorer countries, untreated waste water may flow through ditches, gutters, and open sewers, spreading disease.

People use the open sewer to dump litter and as a handy toilet.

Feces and urine in the sewer contain all kinds of disease bugs.

Body wastes and pools of dirty water get hot in the sun, encouraging bugs to breed.

Heavy rain makes the sewer overflow, spreading wastes and dangerous bugs into the soil and into clean water supplies.

diarrhea runny, loose feces (poop) with lots of fluids

Stinky feet

The soles of your feet are the sweatiest parts of your body (after the palms of your hands). Feet crammed inside socks and shoes create warm, damp, stuffy conditions, perfect for microbes. No wonder feet get so stinky!

Fungi and bacteria love growing in the sweatiest areas, causing problems like athlete's foot.

The area between the toes gets especially sweaty.

Decayed skin reveals raw layers underneath.

Where the athlete's foot fungus digests through the skin, blood and pus ooze out.

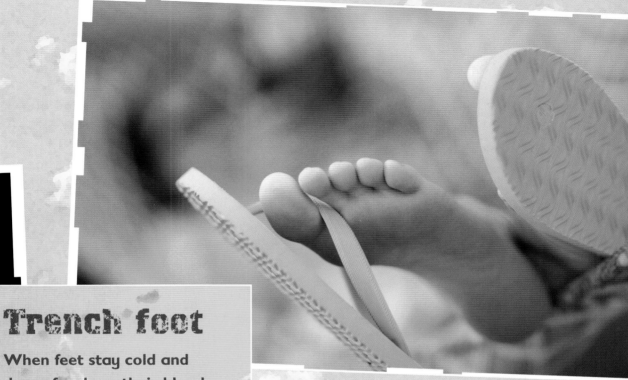

Trench foot

When feet stay cold and damp for days, their blood supply slows, and they become pale and numb. Blisters develop and bacteria start infections. For some soldiers living in trenches in World War I, the flesh rotted, causing **gangrene**. In some cases, the feet had to be **amputated**.

After swimming and sports, avoid athlete's foot by drying feet properly with a clean towel, especially between the toes. Change socks and shoes often. Wear open sandals or flip-flops to keep feet dry and aired.

Athlete's foot, which turns skin into decaying goo, is caused by a fungus—a miniature version of a mushroom or toadstool. Athlete's foot is easy to catch when you share showers or towels with people who have left behind infected flakes of skin.

gangrene death of large areas of body cells   **amputation** cutting off a body part

Glossary

amputation cutting off a body part

anesthetic substance that brings loss of feeling or consciousness

antibody natural bacteria-killing chemical produced by some white blood cells

bacteria common small- to medium-sized microbes

bilharzia serious tropical disease caused by a fluke whose young bore through the skin

bladder bag in the lower body that stores urine (pee)

bug general name for any microscopic or small animal

cells microscopic structures that make up living things

diarrhea loose, runny feces (poop) with lots of fluids

feces person's solid wastes, also called poop

fever high body temperature

gangrene death of large areas of body cells

insect small, six-legged animal with a hard outer casing

malaria dangerous disease caused by one-celled parasites transmitted through mosquito bites

mucus natural body slime that gives a slippery, protective coating

parasite creature that lives in or on another creature and does it harm

pheromone chemical that has a smell that affects other people, without them being aware

plague fast-spreading disease that kills people

plaque mixture of bacteria, saliva, and rotting food that coats teeth and gums

pus pale liquid containing dead blood cells and bacteria

small intestine longest part of the gut, just after the stomach

symptom what a patient feels during an illness

urine person's liquid waste, also called pee

virus tiny bug that causes diseases by invading and killing body cells

Further information

Books

Youch! It Bites! by Trevor Day (Templar Publishing, 2000)
Scary pictures and fascinating facts about animals that bite, stab, or sting you.

Parasites: Latching on to a Free Lunch by Paul Fleisher (Twenty-First Century Books, 2006)
Discover all kinds of parasites, large and small, including parasitic plants.

The Good, the Bad, the Slimy: The Secret Life of Microbes by Sara L Latta (Enslow Publishers, 2006)
Learn how microbes live in and on our bodies, help make food, survive extreme environments, and even change history.

Web sites

FactHound offers a safe, fun way to find Internet sites related to this book. All of the sites on FactHound have been researched by our staff. Visit *www.facthound.com* for age-appropriate sites. You may browse subjects by clicking on letters, or by clicking on pictures and words.
FactHound will fetch the best sites for you!

Films

Fantastic Voyage directed by Richard Fleischer (Twentieth Century Fox, 1966)
People are shrunk in a miniature submarine and injected into a human body. Their amazing adventures include fighting off the attentions of the body's defense system. Parental guidance advised.

Innerspace directed by Joe Dante (Warner Bros, 1987)
With a basic plot similar to *Fantastic Voyage* (above), a test pilot in a submersible craft is miniaturized and passes around the insides of the human body. Parental guidance required.

Index